ANIMAL DADS

Sneed B. Collard III

Illustrated by
Steve Jenkins

Houghton Mifflin Company Boston

Dedicated to Sneed B. Collard Jr.
Through ups and downs, a great father. A great friend.
With love,
III

For my father
—S.J.

For information about this and other Houghton Mifflin trade and reference books and multimedia products, visit The Bookstore at Houghton Mifflin on the World Wide Web at http://www.hmco.com/trade/.

The text of this book is set in Century Old Style.
The illustrations are cut paper collage, reproduced in full color.

Library of Congress Cataloging-in-Publication Data

Collard, Sneed B., III.
Animal dads / by Sneed B. Collard III ; illustrated by Steve Jenkins.
p.   cm.
Summary: Illustrations and simple text describe how the males of different species help take care of their young.
ISBN 0-395-83621-2
1. Parental behavior in animals—Juvenile literature.
[1. Parental behavior in animals.   2. Animals—Habits and behavior.]   I. Jenkins, Steve, 1952– ill.   II. Title.
QL762.C64   1997
591.56—dc20   96-22171   CIP   AC

Manufactured in the United States of America

BVG   10 9 8 7 6 5 4 3 2

Dads do many things.

They build us homes to live in.

A stickleback dad builds a nest out of pieces of plants. The female stickleback lays her eggs in this nest. The male fertilizes them. Afterward the male drives the female away—but his job isn't over yet. Dad continues to guard the nest from enemies, and he protects the babies after they hatch.

They keep us snug and warm.

After an emperor penguin female lays her single egg, she leaves Dad in charge and walks to the sea to search for food. For nine weeks Dad holds the egg on his feet, keeping it warm under a special feather-lined pouch. After the egg hatches, Mom returns. Then, she and Dad take turns feeding and caring for their downy youngster.

They bathe us.

Prairie vole dads share all the duties of raising their kids. They help dig underground nests and tunnels for their babies to live in. They cuddle with their young and keep them warm. When a baby gets dirty, Dad makes sure it gets a good bath.

And just tidy us up.

Gorillas live in close family groups. Dad's main job is to protect the family's territory— but that's not all he does. Sometimes he plays with youngsters and removes biting insects and dirt from their fur. This is called grooming.

Dads watch out for strangers.

Poison-arrow frogs make excellent parents. Some types of female poison-arrow frogs lay their eggs under a stone or in a moist hole. Dad guards these eggs and chases away enemies, including other frogs. After the tadpoles hatch, they wriggle onto Dad's back. Dad carries the tadpoles to a small stream or pond, where they grow into adult frogs.

Like stickleback dads, some cichlid (SIK-LID) fish are active fathers. They build nests, guard eggs, and may even find food for their babies to eat. If danger comes along, some cichlid dads protect their young in an amazing way: Dad opens his mouth and the babies swim inside. The babies stay inside his mouth until the danger has passed.

And shelter us from harm.

They feed us.

Beavers are famous for cutting down trees to build dams and lodges. Beaver dads also cut down trees for another reason. When beaver babies stop drinking mother's milk, Dad chops down trees so the babies can eat meals of fresh, tender bark.

And help us find our voice.

Most birds are born knowing how to sing, but not all. Young male western meadowlarks learn their songs by listening to their dads and other adult males. Young meadowlarks don't always listen to the right songs. Some meadowlarks have learned the songs of red-winged blackbirds, common yellowthroats, and even cardinals!

Sometimes dads play.

Dwarf mongoose dads are good-time dads! Like gorillas, dwarf mongooses live in close families that have aunts, uncles, brothers, sisters, and of course, parents. Mom rarely plays with her youngsters, but Dad often joins in a playful romp in the dirt. Dad also catches most of the food for his youngsters and teaches them how to hunt.

Other times, they perform.

Killdeer lay their eggs on open rocks or gravel. If a predator comes too close to the eggs, a killdeer dad can turn into an actor. Often, he starts shrieking loudly and pretending he has a broken wing. With luck, the predator will follow Dad and leave the killdeer eggs alone.

Dads have their ups . . .

To spawn, or reproduce, salmon
return to the same river or stream
where they were born. The trip
can be difficult. Salmon dads and
moms often have to leap clear out
of the water to get past logs or
rocks. Sometimes, a salmon dad
even wriggles over shallow
stretches of gravel to reach the
place where he will spawn.

Lion dads might seem like lazy dads, but that's not always true. Lions live in family groups called prides. In the pride, female lions raise the cubs and do most of the hunting. Father lions guard the females and cubs and defend the pride's territory from other lions. All of this can be a lot of work. That's why it's not unusual to see a lion dad—yawn!—taking an afternoon nap.

. . . and their downs.

Some dads go away.

Many baby animals never get to
see their parents. After gopher
tortoise dads mate with gopher
tortoise moms, the dads go their
own way. Mom buries her eggs in
a shallow nest in sandy soil. Then
she leaves as well, never to see
her babies after they hatch.

Some dads always stay.

Wolves live together in packs.
Each pack is led by a male and
female wolf, who mate for life.
After a new litter of babies is
born, Dad leads the pack on
hunting trips and brings back
meat for the pups to eat. Dad also
protects the pups, plays with
them, and, of course, teaches
them how to howl.

Dads work with moms.

Like gopher tortoises, most reptile parents leave soon after they have mated and laid their eggs. Nile crocodiles are different. Nile crocodile moms and dads watch over their nests and carry the babies to water after they hatch. Dads also work with moms to chase away predators until the babies can look out for themselves.

And do things for us that we never even know.

Megapodes don't incubate their eggs by sitting on them. Instead, many megapode dads build large mounds of leaves and soil for Mom to lay her eggs in. As the leaves in the mound rot they give off heat, which incubates the megapode's eggs. Mom leaves after she lays the eggs, but Dad sticks around. He turns the leaves over and moves them around to make sure the eggs remain at just the right temperature until they hatch.

Babysitting dads?
You bet.

Tamarins are small primates related to monkeys, gorillas, and people. Tamarins live in groups. Dads often help care for the young—including sharing the babysitting duties. If a curious tamarin youngster wanders away, Dad runs after it and brings it back to the family.

Housecleaning dads?
Sure.

Desert isopod dads and moms dig
and defend the burrows where
they raise their young. Dads also
help with housecleaning. Both he
and Mom carry out soil and
refuse from the burrows. Desert
isopods don't live very long. Both
parents die soon after their young
are born.

Dads that give birth?

It's hard to believe,
but yes. One or two.

After mating, a seahorse or
pipefish mother transfers her
eggs to the father. Inside Dad's
special belly pouch the eggs
hatch, but the young fish don't
swim out right away. They feed
from blood vessels that line Dad's
pouch. When the babies grow big
enough to survive on their own,
Dad gives birth. The babies swim
out into the ocean.

Dads do many things. Dads *are* many things.

0000110657624